Simpler Times

Reflections on Women's Friendship

Kathleen McDonald

WESTBOW°
PRESS
A DIVISION OF THOMAS NELSON
& ZONDERVAN

WestBow Press books may be ordered through booksellers or by contacting:

WestBow Press
A Division of Thomas Nelson & Zondervan
1663 Liberty Drive
Bloomington, IN 47403
www.westbowpress.com
1 (866) 928-1240

Revised Standard Version of the Bible, copyright ©1952 [2nd edition, 1971] by the Division of Christian Education of the National Council of the Churches of Christ in the United States of America. Used by permission. All rights reserved.

Because of the dynamic nature of the Internet, any web addresses or links contained in this book may have changed since publication and may no longer be valid. The views expressed in this work are solely those of the author and do not necessarily reflect the views of the publisher, and the publisher hereby disclaims any responsibility for them.

Any people depicted in stock imagery provided by Thinkstock are models, and such images are being used for illustrative purposes only. Certain stock imagery © Thinkstock.

ISBN: 978-1-4908-6915-5 (sc)
ISBN: 978-1-4908-6917-9 (hc)
ISBN: 978-1-4908-6916-2 (e)

Library of Congress Control Number: 2015901938

Print information available on the last page.

WestBow Press rev. date: 03/02/2015

Contents

Dedication

To my daughters, Becky and Missy,
Friends of My Heart.
May you always know how much you are loved

Acknowledgments

It is with sincere gratitude that I acknowledge the friends who helped me to accomplish this task. Anita Jacobs and Carol von Hagn graciously took time to edit my writing and give me feedback, along with suggestions for improvement. Roxanna Miller read this in its infancy and said, "Well, I just wanted more!" So I obliged her. Ann and Pat Quackenbush suggested that I add discussion and/or reflection questions so it could be used with a group. Virginia Gallagher patiently did technical editing, pointing out things like agreement of margins and spacing, which I never would have thought about. Finally, I thank my dear husband, Richard. He encourages my passion for writing and gives me the quiet time I need to pursue it.

Preface

For a little over ten years of my life, God chose to place me in a truly unique neighborhood. The grace of that time has had a deep-seated effect on my growth as a woman, mother, wife, and Christian. My home was in a small village, on a quiet street filled with old Victorian style houses. Within that lovely assortment of dwellings lived a surprisingly diverse and wide array of interesting women. Most were wives and mothers. Others, who had no children, accepted all of ours as if they were their own.

Times were changing, but in that small corner of the world, if you were a mother, you were at home. So, within a few days of my arrival, I had met most everyone who lived on the street. Within a year's time, I realized that this was a nurturing place where women friends were each other's counselors, helpers, and problem-solvers, as well as the co-parents of our children. I have no doubt today that God placed me in the cocoon of these friendships so I could grow to be the butterfly He wanted me to be.

These women had such a positive impact on my life and the lives of my children that this little book had to be written … not just as a chronicle of my remembrances but also as a tribute to the memory of that simpler time … a time when neighborhoods of women worked together to help build up and strengthen each other. This fine group of women represents a true prototype of the body of Christ at work.

So, I offer to my readers not only reflections and memories but also the wisdom that each woman imparted to me as a gift. Of course, I have changed their names. I have replaced them with names that I feel fit the spiritual impact they had on my life. In our overly rushed world, may these meditations help our hearts and spirits yield to the wisdom of a simpler time.

Wonder

She had a sister named Mary, who sat at the
Lord's feet and listened to what He was saying.
(Luke 10:39 RSV)

A spring day rarely goes by without thoughts of Grace.
Because of her guidance, I learned to experience the wonder
of life and beauty in nature. Soft spring breezes bring her
fragrance into the air around me as the budding flowers
whisper her name. She was a bouquet of fancy words that
voiced poetic splendor, making scenes in my mind that
have lasted through the years.

Grace was a strong, hardy woman with a gentle heart.
Her house resembled Grand Central Station. The coffee was
always on … hot and strong. People milled in and out, and
some stayed for a few days or even a few months. She flowed
through this chaos like a waterfall and handled each crisis
with aplomb. If things became too hectic, she skillfully
ignored the turmoil and went about her business as if no
one was there. She did this with such deftness that she never
made anyone feel uncomfortable. She was just Grace.

We, her neighborhood friends, met all types of interesting
people at her house. She loved to share her guests and would
make sure that we met most of them, from the most natural

everyday types to the truly eccentric. For me, it was a series of lessons in understanding people with widely diverse views and experiences. I learned a great deal about the value of openness—listening to and respecting opinions that differed from mine. This formation tool has helped me immeasurably in dealing with people in the teaching profession as well as in my everyday life.

Although the activity at her house was amazing, the real wonder of Grace was her gift of herself. When the work of mothering or housework became burdensome, any one of us might lift the phone and call Grace. "Got time for coffee?" And with few exceptions, Grace answered, "Yes."

Weather permitting, we usually sat on her back steps and sipped her ever-ready brew. It was coffee—and I mean coffee. It made hair stand on end. A cup of that brew was an assurance that her neighborhood guests would work in full gear the rest of the day. Occasionally, a memory of her coffee makes me chuckle as I anticipate the effect it would have on me now after several years of decaf.

Probably the best part of those coffee breaks was that, while the children played joyfully together, we discussed all kinds of things: the latest book, the news, problems we were facing, new techniques of child care—the list was endless. Grace was so intrigued by ideas. Often she would quiz me on my strong faith, probing to see if it was genuine as she struggled to find where she fit into God's scheme of things. Coffee break over, I'd usually go home refreshed, albeit a bit jittery, and vow that next time I might avoid coffee and have … tea? But … and oh well … it sure was good coffee.

There was no one in our whole neighborhood group that knew more about nature than Grace. She taught me to keep a keen eye for the advent of spring flowers from the moment they peeped through the dark earth until they unfurled into their innate beauty. Because of her personal depth, she saw so much in each new aspect of a plant and shared all of her knowledge. She helped me gather specimens for my first perennial garden.

As a mother, I wanted to share all I learned from Grace with my children. I loved taking my children on walks with her in the fields behind our houses or along the creek that ran through the village. She taught us all about birds and wildflowers. She shared secret paths she had found and taught how to detect animal niches. She instinctively found bunny nests hidden in tufts of weathered hay. We learned to identify various types of ferns. We saw our first feast of marsh marigolds, resplendent in a hidden alcove, a yellow-and-green painting in the spring wetlands. We marveled together at the oddity of plants that decided to grow in unlikely places. These momentary changes in nature's personality became a daily chronicle to share.

Many years have passed, but spring never goes by without nostalgic thoughts of this special woman friend. She helped me to see things in life and in nature that I might have missed if she had not been part of God's plan for my life. Her probing into my spiritual life made me stronger. Her example of openness and sharing increased my awareness. Her availability gave our whole neighborhood a place to rest. Even her caregiving of some of the less fortunate on our street was a testament to her strength of character. We all grew in the network of her love.

Grace, I feel your presence in the spring glow-gathering of light. Thank you for helping me to see.

Prayer

Lord, help us to open our eyes to see the simple, small beginnings that grow into the grace and glory of mature beauty. Let us look at Your gift of nature, as it helps us see how You use the small things of this world to confound the strong. Help us to remember and contemplate how the people You have placed in our lives have been gifted to us. Let us not be so selfish with our time but, like Grace, experience the joy of giving our time to others. Amen.

Reverie

When first spring
Tiptoes slowly 'cross the land,
I wander through my garden.
There, with trained eye,
Amidst the gnarly clods of earth,
I see first evidence of new life breaking ground.
I revel in the mystery that is there
And think of a friend
Long ago and far away
Who …
With her loving eye could see it all
And shared her vision so my eyes could understand
The beauty of beginnings
That graced the waiting land.
In memory's mind I see her.
Her blessing fills the air.
In quiet contemplation,
It seems she's standing there.

Questions to contemplate or discuss:

1. How open am I to the opinions of others? Do I listen, or do I immediately close my mind? How can I compare myself to Jesus in the way I treat those who disagree with me?
2. How do I respond to interruptions in my day? Who is in charge of my time? Is it myself or is it God?
3. Is there a Grace in my life? When was the last time I remembered to thank her?
4. Have I been a Grace to others?

Scripture readings/reflections:

1. Philemon
2. Psalm 104
3. Ephesians 2:4–10

Something to do:

Take a walk on the next sunny or clear day. Concentrate on nature—the growing things, the flying things, and the sounds. Write a reflection or a poem about what you see or hear. Share it with a friend.

Personal Reflections

Service

There, [in Bethany] they gave a dinner for Him
[Jesus] and Martha served. (John 12:2 RSV)

Just down the street in a long white house with perfectly
manicured flowerbeds lived a busy little lady called Julia.
Though tiny in stature, her energy level at eighty put most of
us to shame. She was a retired teacher. She and her husband
had no children, so they adopted the neighborhood world
around them as family.

Julia rarely rested and always used her many God-given
talents. She shared her quilting, sewing, and delicious
cooking with others. In charge of the church rummage sale,
she prepared the leftover items to be sent to the missions.
However, she did not just pack the clothing up and send
it off; she spent hours patching and mending the items to
make them usable gifts. It was not uncommon to see her
slipping out of her house with a basket filled with freshly
cooked food for someone who was sick, bedridden, or in
mourning. She did all of this charitable work as quietly as
possible and was uncomfortable when one of us caught her
at her tasks.

This spunky little lady had a nice word for everyone

and was always ready with encouragement. On Wednesday nights, several of us walked to a nonsectarian Christian Bible study and prayer group. Julia went with us. She was our oldest member. On the way, we young mothers vented about the joys and woes of the day as we'd juggled one child's needs against another's. Julia, in the meantime, was in constant pain from the severe spurs in her feet, but she never complained. Instead, she spent the whole walk encouraging us. She lifted our spirits, and only once do I remember her even mentioning how much her poor feet hurt.

Julia was always in a hurry. One day I was in a Christian bookstore with my friend Sophie. Actually, we were sitting on the floor perusing a number of books. I picked up a copy of Hannah Hurnard's classic *Hinds' Feet on High Places.*

"You know," I said. "I never can keep a copy of this book. Every time I get one, I end up giving it away."

At that very moment, Julia whisked into the store. She walked straight for us and said, "You know, I came in here for a book. It's that one you are always telling me to read, and for the life of me, I can't remember its name."

"Is it this one?" I asked.

"Oh yes! That is just it!"

I handed the book to her, and she went straight to the checkout, purchased the book, and was gone almost before Sophie and I could close our mouths. We laughed many times about that little incident. It was a sure example of how God provides for our needs as well as an endearing little moment in our relationship with Julia.

Julia taught me to be Jesus to others, to lift people up and to see the best in them. She exemplified how to use our gifts to enhance the lives of others. Whenever I hurt from my own physical problems, I remember her quiet suffering and how she never let anything stop her. I'm not sure that I will move as quickly in my eighties as she did, but I am determined to try.

Today, Julia is with the Lord. She lived to be over one hundred, struggling in her last years with Parkinson's disease. Despite her discomfort, she still wrote me an annual Christmas letter. In it, she encouraged me as well as remembered special times we had shared in our little neighborhood. I am sure she was a delight at the nursing home where she spent her last years.

Julia, thank you for your example ... it nourishes
me like a healthy balm and provides proper
shame when I complain too much.

Prayer

Lord, what a wonder Your Marthas are. They are there almost before the tragedies happen … antennas tuned to Your Holy Spirit. They move at breakneck speed and seem ever ready to do what needs to be done. I am not like that, Lord. It takes me time … sometimes too long, and the opportunity passes. Let me appreciate the whirlwinds of this world more than I do and to understand them a little better. Help those of us who are introspective to pray for them more. Then, we may have a part in their gift of taking care of things swiftly and on time. Amen

Small Wonder

Tiny little lady, busy as a bee,
Trying hard to make the world
The way it ought to be.
A thoughtful word, a whispered prayer
So simply shared each day.
A little sweet encouragement
Dropped along the way.
Reflection of our savior's life
On earth
For all to see,
Tiny little lady,
Example set for me.

Questions to contemplate or discuss:

1. When I look at myself, do I see a Martha or a Mary ... or a combination of both?
2. As a Martha, how willing am I to accept the Marys around me? Do I pressure them to do more, or am I able to learn from their different approach to life?
3. As a Mary, do I feel intimidated by the Marthas around me, or do I appreciate the good they accomplish?
4. How *quiet* am I about my service? Do I need to be seen or am I satisfied to be a *silent servant*?
5. Who is the Martha in my life? Have I thanked her recently?

Scriptures readings/reflections

1. Luke 10:38–42
2. Proverbs 31:10–31
3. Psalm 27

A note to write:

Find a lovely card and your favorite pen, and curl up in a comfy chair. Write a note to a Martha in your life and thank her for all she does.

Personal Reflections

Determination

> But Ruth said, "Do not press me to leave you
> or to turn back from following you! Where
> you go I will go ..." (Ruth 1:16 RSV)

When my neighbor, Ruth, was in her thirties, she had a stroke. It paralyzed a good part of her left side so that she walked with a pronounced limp, had little use of her arm, and lived with a deformed face. Through sheer determination, she learned to function with surprising vigor despite her disabilities.

When I met her, she was well into her sixties and lovingly cared for, not only by her husband, but also by all the members of this remarkable neighborhood community. She was predictable, faithful, and relentless in spirit, though she sometimes gave us worry headaches at her antics, such as going out on the icy sidewalks alone. She was truly a part of our God-given responsibilities.

Ruth started every morning by making her rounds. She went to the post office. Then, on her way back, she stopped at every neighbor's house for a visit. Some days she was full of woe as she dealt with an immature adult child who was a constant drain on her energy. Other times, she was full of business, telling us what was on sale at the nearby grocery store. I always got a chuckle about the number of chuck roasts she'd bring home when they were on sale. She must have used every recipe for chuck roast available to man. Of course, *at that price*, they were just too lovely to pass up. Some mornings she took it upon herself to insist on helping according to the plan *she* had in mind for *my* day.

I tended to let my mail and paperwork pile up. With four toddlers, time was precious, and checking bills and advertisements was low on my priority list. I always put this precarious assortment on the top of the dishwasher. Ruth could take this for only so long. She would come in, make herself a cup of tea or coffee, and say, "Now, this mess has been neglected long enough. I am just going to sit here and keep an eye on things until you get this mail taken care of." And that she would do.

Needless to say, Ruth could be a curse or a blessing to all of her neighborhood friends depending on our moods. If Ruth decided that one of us should do a job, we knew that our plans for the day would have to change. She would just sit there until we did her bidding. Alas, old habits are hard to break, and now sometimes I wish she'd pop down from above when I get behind. I still have a clutter problem, and when I work on it, I often picture her sitting patiently watching me straighten things up.

Although married, I was alone with my little ones most of the time. My kind neighbors took special care of my needs and watched over my family lovingly. Canning time was Ruth's own special organized effort to make things easier for me.

"Well," she'd say matter-of-factly, "It looks like it is time for tomatoes, (or pears ... or beans). I will be here at eight tonight."

Promptly at eight, while I was upstairs finishing baths, saying prayers, and tucking my children in for the night, I would hear action in the kitchen. By the time I got downstairs, everything was set up. Usually she had recruited four or five of the neighbors, some to help, some to coach, and some just to watch and visit. We'd work and laugh, sweat and slave together. At the end of the evening, we'd all sit down exhausted, but there on the sideboard would be fifteen or twenty jars of canned goods.

Ruth's only true failure as my *canning coach* was the day she decided to teach me how to make grape jelly. "You just can't waste all these grapes. Why, with your children, you need lots of jelly." Three or four of the crew were in the kitchen that day. The children had been relegated to the care of my *Over the Back Fence* friend, Katherine. I had all kinds of help, but with all the varied advice, the task was ultimately destined for disaster. I, impetuously, didn't listen well to the straining directions from my myriad teachers. I squeezed the cheesecloth filled with grapes with great vigor and grapes flew everywhere. We were all covered with grape skins and juice. We laughed until tears ran down our faces, ready to give up on the whole thing.

Not so for Ruth. She never wasted anything. In fact, she had such a stockpile of food supplies that I think we could all have lived in her cellar for a year after a natural disaster. Thus, she was not going to call it a day. She was determined to save what was possible. The grape jelly was going to be completed.

She put all of us to the task of saving what remained. When we finished, it was the most disgusting looking jelly I have ever seen. There were little pieces of skin dotting the overcooked clear gel. It took me forever to get to the last of it, as my children, who would usually eat anything, looked skeptical whenever I opened a jar of that *stuff*. Never again have I attempted grape jelly, but Ruth's unrelenting spirit was good for the soul. No wonder she survived a stroke!

∾

My house was a kind of prayer center. People often stopped throughout the day for prayer or to share some spiritual experience. For Ruth, this was a regular need in her life. Several of us convinced her to attend our Bible study. She felt uncomfortable at first because she wasn't a reader, but her fear was quenched when we assured her that she didn't have to read unless she wanted to. So she came and loved those who loved her back. At home, she haltingly started to read Scripture to herself. Before long, as she felt more comfortable with the group, she began to volunteer to read passages. It was a joy to see.

One of my fondest memories involving Ruth was the first time she finished reading a whole book. It was a spiritual book that we were sharing in our Bible study group. Due to her stroke, she had stopped reading as she could not remember what she read. So when she came over, thrilled, and told me all about this book that she had understood and remembered, I knew God had worked a miracle for her … a miracle for all of us. After that, she often had a book in hand and proudly stopped by to share new bits of information.

Ruth taught me much about determination and the ability to keep going despite physical drawbacks. She had her own longing to be loved, and we, as neighbors, provided the nurturing she needed to feel accepted and encouraged. She took pride in being our busy helper, teaching me that keeping busy keeps one's mind off the difficulties that we have to endure.

Most of all, she showed that coming close to God can create a life that blossoms like a beautiful garden. As she grew to know Him more, not only did she discover the world of reading, but also the glow of her growth shone in her face. That beauty replaced her deformity in the eyes of those who loved her.

Now, Ruth is home with the Lord. I would not be surprised if she is trying to set His schedule too.

Thank you, Ruth, for teaching me the patience to endure. Thank you for demonstrating to me what determination it takes to be an overcomer.

Prayer

Dear Lord, help us to see You in all, especially those whose disabilities and pain-filled bodies sometimes frighten us. Let us see the love they offer us in their selfless ways, as they, in turn, hope for our nurturing love. Bless us with Your sight that sees beyond the physical into the beauty of the heart. With this newfound awareness, may we be a shield of light and protection for them. Amen.

The Gift Giver

Through so many years of twisted pain
I've had to walk, Lord,
With people laughing ... dreading me,
And then you put me here
In this safe haven
Where, with angel wings around me
To protect,
I've learned to grow ... to glow in you.
With all my quirks, friends hold my hand
To help me walk with pride again.
I know they sometimes tire
Of my persistence, demanding time
From them each day.
But, Lord, may these special people remember me
As one whose determination touched their lives
With my own brand of help ...
My recipe of love.

Questions to contemplate or discuss:

1. How do I respond to people deformed by illness, accident, or birth defect? Do I look at them with the eyes of Jesus?
2. How aware am I of their need for love and their longing for acceptance?
3. Who in my life is Ruth? What can she teach me? How can I be Christ to her?
4. Am I aware of the needs of young mothers who have to raise their children alone? What can I do to help?

Scripture readings/reflections:

1. Luke 8:43–48
2. Mark 2:1–12

A story to read:

"The Happy Prince," by Oscar Wilde, a timeless classic about self-giving love.

Personal Reflections

Humor

You show me the path of life. In your presence
there is fullness of joy. (Psalm 16:11 RSV)

Next door, in an old stone house, lived a dear old lady
named Anna. She patiently waited out the years of old age
with laughter and the ability to mock her maladies. She
taught our little neighborhood community much about
getting the most out of life in the later years. Anna was
close enough so that I could sit on her *stoop*, as she called
it, and visit while my children played in the backyard. But
as often as not, she would appear in my backyard to visit
while I hung the clothes or tended the garden.

Well into her eighties, she could stand and visit for so
long that it put me to shame. She remained standing long
after I had given up. I, the *young* mom, plopped down on
a spot in the grass or on a nearby step, gazing up at this
resilient icon. To me, it was a remarkable natural ability. It
took me many more years and a course in tai chi to even
come close to standing for half the time she could.

I remember Anna for her wonderful sense of humor as
well as her resilience. She laughed at her physical problems
and scoffed at her *senior moments*. One day Anna decided to

heat a leftover zucchini casserole. Instead of taking out the Tupperware saver with the zucchini in it, she accidentally took out a similar container that stored an exotic type of fishermen's bait that her husband had purchased for his next fishing trip. She warmed the whole thing up in a pan, divided it in two helpings and set it before her man. Needless to say, her husband immediately recognized the concoction and was not amused.

"It looked just the same," she reasoned. "You'd think he'd know better than to put his fishing stuff right in the refrigerator with the food." She couldn't stop laughing when she told her tale and reveled in the funny incident to the chagrin of her husband. We all joined in her hilarity.

One day she came over to tell me that she had an aneurysm and would be going in for surgery as soon as possible. The doctor had told her to be very careful not to jostle herself. The aneurysm was in a dangerous place where one wrong move could be the end. She was scared. We talked for some time, and she was feeling better.

So, when she left, I said, "Let me walk you down the steps, because I don't want you to fall."

So, we started off down the back porch steps. My old Victorian home was a repair job in progress. When we got to the third step, it collapsed, and there we were tumbling off to the ground together. I was in a panic as I looked around to see if Anna was alive. She took one look at me and burst out laughing.

"You should see the look on your face, Kathy. I'm okay. Now maybe your steps will be fixed."

That was Anna, wise enough to see the humor in the most ironic situation. Thank God, she did make it to the hospital in one piece … no thanks to her neighbor. To make the story even more miraculous, my steps were *finally* fixed.

Another time, at one of our neighborhood nighttime canning sessions, she brought over a couple of big pots and some serrated spoons. As these evenings were always fun-filled, we started kidding her about being the oldest one there. She shot back her usual barbs, and when it was time to leave, we dared her to wear her pan collection home. Without pause, she put one pan on her head, used another as a drum, and paraded down the street with glee. I can still see the delight in her face and the laugh wrinkles about her eyes.

Of course, even those with the gift of humor can't be all laughter. She had some pretty sad things to deal with. At times, she depended on us to listen to her worries and cares. She soaked in strength from us to deal with serious health problems, depending on our encouragement and prayer. Her husband was difficult to live with and always saw the hole in the doughnut. She'd learned to cope with his moods and taught me the meaning of constant forgiveness in dealing with my own marital problems.

In exchange for filling the void in her loneliness, she gave her neighborhood friends … she called us all *young things* … her time, wisdom, and her laughter.

After I moved away, I enjoyed sending her silly cards. At that time, Boynton's witty cards and sayings were popular. I found one with a man crawling through the underbrush based on the Livingstone and Stanley story. Inside it said, "Living still, I presume." I knew it would make her laugh, so I sent it to her with a giggle. She died a few days later. At first I felt awful about the card and my *sick* humor. Then I thought of her laughing from heaven at my blunder, and it became one of my fun stories to tell.

Anna's undaunted desire to maintain a good attitude toward her age and her circumstances has walked with me through the pages of life and remains with me daily.

> Thank you, Anna, for your gift of laughter. Thank you for always being there and watching over my little family from your next-door stoop.

Prayer

Lord, growing older seems to sneak up on us. We see it in little changes here and there. Then suddenly, we look in the mirror and say, "Is that really me?" Help us to grow old gracefully and keep a good attitude with a large measure of humor. Help us to laugh at ourselves and enjoy each moment as a gift from You.

And Lord, while we are getting there ourselves, help us to be mindful of the elderly. Let us listen to their stories, glean knowledge from their wisdom, and give of our time to help fulfill their longing for love and care. Amen.

In a Mind's Eye

I still see you sitting there,
Wrinkled from years of wear,
Eyes twinkling,
Observing the daily drone of young families
Frantically fussing about.

Legs crossed with cup of tea in hand,
Hoping for some company to fill the long, lonely day …
To share maladies punctuated with humor-sense,
Or muse about seasons, and some newfound recipe,
Living in the present while sharing wisdom
From longtime years of growth.

To peak around the side of my porch
And see you there
Was enduring assurance
Of things that would always be.
In my mind you stay … reminding,
Always reminding me,
To take each day for what it brings my way.

Questions to contemplate or discuss:

1. Who is the oldest person in my neighborhood? When was the last time I visited with him or her? Have I offered to do something helpful?
2. Do I seek wisdom from the elderly? Do I acknowledge that they may have valuable experiences to share?
3. What role do I play as an older person in my neighborhood? Am I willing to share myself with the young mothers around me? Am I patient with the children?
4. Do I have an Anna in my life? What gifts has she given me?

Scriptures readings/reflections

1. Luke 2:36–38
2. Genesis 21:1–8
3. Proverbs 15:13 and 16:16

A lighthearted book to read:

Walking Across Egypt, by Clyde Edgerton.
This delightful book about age and youth will make you laugh.

Personal Reflections

38

Compassion

For He shall give his angels charge over you, to
keep you in all your ways. (Psalm 91:11 NKJV)

The members of the body that seem to be weaker
are indispensable … If one member suffers, all
suffer together with it. (1 Corinthians 12:22
and 12:26a RSV)

Across the street and kitty-corner from my house, lived
my friend, May. She suffered from periodic bouts of severe
depression. As she spent much of her time in and out of
hospitals, I am sure she was placed in the safe cocoon of our
neighborhood because of her needs.

We all had our particular role in her care. Some offered
encouragement, bolstering up her self-image and supporting
her with words. Others prayed for her relentlessly. A large
group kept an eye on her young children and gave words of
guidance to her older ones. The more assertive of us made sure
she took her medicine, while others were attuned to the first
signs that she was losing touch with reality.

My memories of May are gentle ones. She was such a
generous soul. She wanted everything to be proper: her house
in order, the right clothes on her children, and always—yes,

always—correct speech. Much of her world existed in her mind, which was surely part of her illness. She would come to visit and share her latest plans. Usually they included things that just seemed impossible like redoing her whole house, buying all new furniture, or some other masterful change. Oddly enough, she would find some way to complete these plans. It was almost like she envisioned these total changes as a reconstruction of herself … the one thing with which she couldn't cope. During these times, she would discard amazingly lovely things. I used one of her gorgeous mahogany tables for years. Then, almost like clockwork, when she completed her new endeavor, she would be gone from us … not physically, but mentally.

One or more of us would notice her walking about in a kind of trance … up and down the street. We'd try to get her to take her medicine, but to no avail. Then she would close her door and shut out the world. Her children ran free, and it was our responsibility to take turns watching over the little ones until a relative would finally arrive to care for them. May would then return to a mental health facility.

Never once did May admit to her illness. She would be gone for a while and return like nothing happened. Then over time, she would repeat the refrain, moving from health back into the dark morass that her mind created for her. We could only offer our love and support in simple ways. While we wanted to make it all right for her, I think that the world that she made up did in some way take her to a dimension within with which she could deal.

May's husband came from a very wealthy family who eventually took charge and changed May's future entirely.

During one of her hospital stays, the in-laws moved their son home with them, took the children, and easily got custody of them. Her house was sold, and they provided an apartment for her. They probably never had any understanding of the care she received on a daily basis from her neighborhood support group. We met that day with a mixture of sadness and relief. We all loved May but knew that she couldn't continue on such an unstable path with several children to raise.

Without her realization, she taught me many lessons. In the constant frenzy of parenting and dealing with my own problems, she blessed me with the knowledge that reality, as imperfect and hard as it can sometimes be, is a great blessing. She helped nurture in my heart a lifelong seed of compassion for the mentally challenged as well as a seeing eye into the lives of families who live and suffer because of such illness. In my subsequent return to teaching, May's presence in my mind helped me provide a safe haven for young children from dysfunctional homes.

Several years ago, I received a letter from May. She was looking for all of her old neighbors. The letter was wistful and sounded so like her. I answered but never heard back. My hope is that she is somewhere wrapped in the special blanket of God's love.

> May, gentle like the spring flowers, thank you
> for seeing the possibilities that dreams afford
> while teaching me that reality is a gift.

Prayer

Dear Lord, thank You for this real day. Help us in our impatient rush to recognize what a great gift life is. Lead us to have compassion and understanding for the people in the body of Christ who are frail and cannot cope. Let us be Christ to them … to love them so that in their dark sadness, they can somehow feel Your love and reach out, through that love, for Your hand. Amen

In the Darkness

I wander through this dark world of sad.
What are these strains of noise around me?
Calling,
Calling me back,
To a muddle-time world
I cannot make sense of.
Quiet … don't you see?
Nothing there is real to me.
It isn't perfect there,
And that I cannot bear.
So leave me here,
Away
And lost to thee.
I sense your love and care
But cannot come.
I grasp at life, but cannot seem
To hold on anymore.
Deep compassion? I do feel it,
Somehow, someway, someday
I may learn to make life real.

Questions to contemplate or discuss:

1. In this twenty-first century work-world society, how aware am I of my neighbors? Would I know if someone close by needed special care or help?
2. If there is a May in my life, have I read up on the illness she suffers? Do I find myself judging her situation or am I looking for ways to help?
3. In many cases, work friends have replaced neighborhood friends. How do I treat a coworker who is mentally challenged?
4. Do I provide love and support for the children of mentally-impaired adults?

Scripture Readings/Reflections:

1. Romans 12:3–21
2. Galatians 5:22–26
3. Psalm 88 and 89

A compassionate novel to read:

The Penny, by Joyce Meyer

Personal Reflections

Wisdom

She opens her mouth with wisdom and
the teaching of kindness is on her tongue.
(Proverbs 31:26 RSV)

In my jewelry box, I have a stickpin and earrings with an
iris design on them ... a treasure from my dear friend,
Sophie, who lived across the creek from me. A bed of irises
banked this little rivulet that wound its way between our
homes. This flower garden was the perfect frame for Sophie's
rambling old Victorian house.

I can still see her standing beneath the picturesque
mantle of trees in her yard calling, "Good Morning!" and
"Let's get together for a chat" as she watched me give final
outdoor play instructions to my little brood.

"Give me an hour," I'd call. "I need to get the dishes
done, make the beds, and get some laundry started."

"Sounds good," she'd reply.

As the neighborhood gathering of kids filled my
backyard, I'd watch from the window and get my chores
done. Then, I'd *rock-step* across the stream of water and
knock on Sophie's door. Her home mirrored her cozy, warm
personality and reflected the comfort and wisdom that she
offered as her gift to our little neighborhood. A lifetime of

memories was garnered as I sat in my *special* chair at her kitchen table.

The first moment I met Sophie, I knew we were kindred spirits. The sparkle in her eyes and the smile wrinkles that ran like small rivulets along her face drew me to her at once. Laughter flowed freely between us. Laughter is such a healing gift and always lends a sense of freedom.

We also had many soulful conversations that helped us grow within ourselves, as friends and as Christians. Sometimes when we became too reflective, one of us would lighten the air with some absolutely foolish remark, and we'd laugh ourselves silly.

Sophie was the comfort giver in our midst. An introspective person herself, she seemed always attuned to the inner workings of her friends' hearts. At just the right time, she'd offer that little golden nugget of encouragement … saying just the right words to make her listener think or act. She gently chided us if needed, but always with wisdom beyond her age. She knew when to just sit quietly and listen. I loved the stubborn look on her face when she was about to tell me to *shape up* about some worry or concern that she knew I could deal with. Sophie's wisdom grew from instinctive empathy, but when she put her hands on her hips and started to talk, I knew I was *in for it*.

While comforting wisdom was her gift, nurturing was her vocation. Two children and a kind husband were her main occupations. When it came to her family, she was like a lioness guarding her lair or a broody hen over her chicks. Our neighborhood family trusted her advice precisely because we saw the fruits of her labors in her fine family. Her parenting skills were a daily model for all of us. Sophie's motherly spirit also drew our motley crew of children to her. She was like the pied piper, and it wasn't just because of her wonderful cookies either … although they helped.

Sophie taught me how to deal with pain. Her body was compromised by serious back problems, which over the years moved like a creeping fungus throughout other parts of her body. She met each new physical crisis with determination. Strong willed, but trusting in the Lord to give her courage, she prevailed. Often I would wake up in the night and feel led to pray for her, and then, in the morning I'd find out she'd had a particularly difficult night. Her positive attitude toward pain was an invaluable gift to me that I incorporate into my daily life.

Sophie was wise, but she was also stubborn. It wasn't hard to figure out when she was struggling with a dilemma. All of a sudden, she would detach from everyone and take a few days alone to puzzle and pray. When she felt satisfied with a course of action, she'd be back to her old self like a reinserted light bulb. It was her unique way of problem solving, but again a valuable lesson. Instead of grumbling to everyone, she let the struggle be hers and the Lord's.

In my own life, Sophie was a bridge of strength during a time when I was trying to cope with a difficult personal situation. The children and I became part of her family, and that in itself gave me a feeling of safety and security. She kept constant vigilance over us like an angel. Although God gave me an unwavering faith, He knew, in His wisdom, that I needed someone understanding right next door during some heartrending times. Her guidance was instrumental in giving me the courage to leave my secure niche of friends and start a new life when the Lord stepped in and called the children and me to a new community.

Psalm 139 is one of my favorite psalms. I love the feeling that God knows my innermost being, and He is there even before I know what I am going to do. It is a rare gift when an earthly friend really knows who we are down deep in the depths of our being. I have been privileged to have such a friend. I use the gift of her wisdom every day of my life. Jesus, the lover of my soul, gave me Sophie as my earthly Psalm 139 friend.

Thank you, Sophie, my wise friend, for adding so much color to the little body of Christ in our neighborhood and for being a true heart friend.

Prayer

Dear Father in heaven, help us to be aware … to listen … to hear with our hearts as well as our ears. Use us to reach others, bringing Your wisdom as we listen to the Holy Spirit instructing us. Let us learn the value of home and family so we can nourish this world with the strength of love. Most of all, Lord, let us be aware of the people You place in our lives along the way who enrich us and help us to reach out for the place You want us to be. In the name of Your dear Son, Jesus, I pray. Amen.

Warm Memories

Wonder-warm kitchen,
Rocking chair near,
Good friends 'round the table
Bringing good cheer.
Sun streams through the windows,
Mugs full of brew,
Cookie smells wafting
As chatter ensues.
Children are playing;
Their laughs fill the air.
Good memories beckon,
Shutting out cares.
Hearts full of love,
Friendship so true,
When I think of these moments,
I think, friend, of you.

Questions to contemplate or discuss:

1. Do I allow laughter to bring release to pent-up emotions, or do I separate joy and suffering?
2. How do I problem solve? Do I do it along with the Lord, or do I find it easier to talk to someone and hear myself dealing with the problem?
3. Is there a Sophie in my life? When was the last time I let her know how meaningful her friendship is to my growth and development?
4. How often do I discern the presence of wisdom in the conversations or actions of my friends?

Scripture readings/reflections:

1. 1 Samuel 18:1–4; 19:4–7; 20:9–17
2. Proverbs 2:1–12
3. 1 John 4:7–21

A story to read:

I'll Love You Forever, by Robert Munsch.
You may want to buy this book for your whole family because it is so touching … warm with wisdom.

Personal Reflections

The In and Outers

> For just as the body is one and has many members, and all the members of the body, though many, are one body, so it is with Christ ... Indeed the body does not consist of one member but of many. (1 Corinthians 12:12, 14 RSV)

Modern society is always in flux. It was not unusual that our little upstate New York community included families who came, left their mark, and moved on. A few of them took up their residence on our street. Each of the following women touched my life in some definable way. I can trace their influence through little memory-sparks that flit through my heart.

Emma—the Worker

Emma lived in the oldest house in our little village. Ironically she was the most avant-garde of any of us. She believed in the *simple* life and did everything in the *natural* way. She gardened, organically of course, and baked, sewed, and spun. She was a passionate environmentalist, a strident advocate of women's rights, and a vocal anti-war protestor.

Her fervor for politics was catching, and she kept us all

on our toes about current events. When we had a differing opinion from hers, we needed to be sure we were well read on the subject. She even got me to go door-to-door to have a petition signed. I don't remember what it was for, but will never forget doing it, as it was so uncharacteristic of me. She made us *put our money where our mouths were*. It was fun having her around, and her spark lit up the street. I still think of her when I see anyone with a long braid or hear a radical opinion.

Emma's dedication to what she believed and her kindness to all, old and young, gave her magnetism. She accepted people where they were at without conditions ... a good lesson. I also thank her for sharing her knowledge about good foods and organic gardening. I started my own quest toward healthy eating at a young age due to her example.

Not surprisingly, her husband finished his doctorate, and they moved to a college campus where he became a professor. When she left, we all made a square that was placed in a homemade quilt that delighted her. I am sure she is at rallies and marches even today. At least I hope she has not lost her strong desire to change the world for the better.

Lenora—the Lady

Lenora was quite old when I first met her. She was very much a lady and reminded me of a Victorian matron. Her house was decorated with frills and doilies, which, more than words, gave voice to her personality.

My family moved into our home just a few days before I had my third child. My mother was with me for a week after the birth so I could get some rest, and on the day that Lenora came, I was fast asleep. Mom was out back doing some laundry, and the little ones were napping. I heard the doorbell ring and foggily wandered to the door. There stood a sweet, stately form that welcomed me to the neighborhood and asked to see my new baby.

"What baby?" I replied in my fog.

The poor woman was struck dumb with shock and stuttered something like, "Well … I thought … I … I …"

Then, like a fool, I made matters worse and said, "Oh! *That* baby."

Well, needless to say, with my foot plunged deeply down my throat I led her in to see my special treasure. I was fully awake by then … and tinted a bright red. After she left, my mom and I laughed until the tears flowed.

From that day forward, Lenora viewed me with skeptical reserve. I tried to turn the story into a neighborhood joke so she wouldn't question my motherly deftness, but to no avail. I had offended her sensibilities.

It is easy to see what I learned from Lenora … to *think before you speak.*

Lucy—the Light-Spirited

One home on our street was always rented to Navy families who attended the nearby college. Lucy stayed in our neighborhood for several years, and unlike many of the tenants who kept to themselves, she immersed herself in our lives. She was friendly and thoughtful.

I knew her for only a short time, but her generosity left an indelible mark on my memory. When I had my fourth child, she figured that most of my baby things were pretty worn out and lavished me with several welcome hand-me-downs. The one I used and appreciated most was a lovely carriage. It was such a blessing to me. I was so busy, and it was wonderful to put my little one out under a tree for a nap while I worked in the garden, hung the wash, or watched the children play. Over the years, I think of Lucy gratefully whenever this so welcome gift flutters back into my memory.

I'd known few military families at that time in my life. Theirs was a foreign world to me. I was aware that they moved a lot, but until getting to know Lucy, I never realized how flexible they had to be. Lucy loved our neighborhood, but she was able to pull up roots and move on when the time came. She had unwavering support for her husband's career. She helped me to respect the sacrifices made by military families as well as the good nature many of the wives and children must nurture to have a life of constant change.

Lucy loved to laugh, so she was naturally drawn to Sophie. When Lucy left, she *gave me permission* to be friends with Sophie because, "You laugh enough to be her friend." Sophie and I laughed over my inheritance many times over the years. I am sure Lucy moved about many more times until her husband reached retirement. I hope she is finally settled in one place, just as she is settled in a spot in the memory of my heart.

∿

The *In and Outers* were wisps of the wind of the Holy Spirit in my life and valuable gifts. I just love the way God chooses people to open our eyes to things we might have never known or understood without His intervention.

Thank you, Emma, Lenora, and Lucy for passing through my life and enriching it.

Prayer

Lord, so many people pass through our lives. Often they are gone before we have time to catch up with the gift they have been. Help us always to be open to each person and alert to what You teach us through them. There is so much to learn and so little time. Thank You for bringing Yourself to us through others. Amen.

God's Flower Garden

Some step through our lives,
While some come to stay.
Each whispers a message
In her own special way.
We can hear or reject it.
We can grow or stand still
On the roads that we wander
As we walk in God's will.
If we look for His message
In all whom we meet,
We will grow like a flower,
Fragrant and sweet.

Questions to contemplate or discuss:

1. In this busy twenty-first century, how aware are you of the people who move in and out of our neighborhoods?
2. Do I consider myself to be close-minded or open-minded? Do I keep out people who don't agree with me? Do I see each person as a unique individual loved by God?
3. How often do I think of the hardships of families in the military? If I am a peace advocate, do I treat military people with respect?
4. We have Lenoras in our lives … maybe an eccentric neighbor, or the lady down the street who has dedicated her life to caring for a disabled family member. Who is Lenora for you? Is she perhaps lonely?

Scripture readings/reflections:

1. Matthew 2:13–15; 19–23
2. 1 John 4:16–21
3. Proverbs 3:27–30

A children's book to read:

A Single Shard, by Linda Sue Park, winner of the Newberry Medal. I picked this book because one of its poignant lessons was that a tiny piece of a valuable object can reflect the beauty of the whole. The women in *The In and Outers* were offered to our neighborhood for such a short time, but gave tiny pieces of wisdom that were molded together into the *clay* of our lives.

Personal Reflections

Around the Fringes

I thank my God every time I remember you, constantly praying with joy in every one of my prayers for all of you because of your sharing in the gospel from the first day until now. I am confident of this, that the one who began a good work among you will bring it to completion by the day of Christ Jesus. (Philippians 1:3–6 RSV)

Neighborhoods, like the body of Christ, are not just made up of the people who live there; they also include the people who wander in and out on a periodic basis. Some bring the fresh fruits of new wisdom, and some come to be sustained by the blanket of love that they feel when they enter a sacred space. Our neighborhood was a welcoming beacon to many, and a few stand out because of the gift they were in my life. What they taught stays in my memory like a wonderful book that holds an honored spot on my bookcase ... a book waiting to be read again and again.

The Fleece

Lois lived on a farm outside of the village. She delighted children with her horses and her llamas. Whenever able to get away, she'd join us at Bible study. She depended on our prayers for her slowly failing eyesight. She had a degenerative condition, and at the time, she could see fairly well in the day, but at night or in dim light, she was almost blind. God used her eye problem to work a wonder in my life.

Lois had been a member of Al-Anon (a support group for the spouses, families, and friends of alcoholics) for many years. A dear family member of mine was struggling with an addiction to alcohol. My sister, who lived in another area, had dealt with it by joining Al-anon and wanted me to do the same. Friends also encouraged me to talk to Lois about Al-Anon. I was not only hesitant, but a bit frightened, wondering what the consequences of sharing a family problem with strangers would be. I wasn't sure I'd have the courage to tell my husband that I was going to a support group as he thought my worries were unfounded.

One day, I hired a babysitter so I could take a walk into the village by myself. I decided to go to the library. I was browsing in the children's section when I saw Lois drive up and park outside. She loved to read and read as much as possible as her impending blindness loomed like a specter.

The library was in an historic old building. The front rooms were light and filled with windows, while the back rooms were poorly lit. So, like Gideon, I threw out a fleece. "Lord," I said, "if I am supposed to go to Al-Anon, let Lois find me in the darkest row in the back room of the library."

I hightailed it into a hiding place and held my breath. The chances of Lois coming back where I *innocently* browsed were minimal. I hoped beyond hope that she'd stay where she belonged … in the front room.

I could hear her talking to the librarian and asking for a book. "I know right where that book is," the librarian said. "I know you won't be able to see it, so if you just wait a minute, I'll get it for you."

They started discussing some local matters while I held my breath. It was obvious that the book was in one of the back rooms.

"Okay. Let me get that book for you," the librarian said, and they continued to talk. I heard the librarian approaching and realized that Lois was following her, chatting along the way. I tried to place myself as close to the bookshelf as possible hoping to blend in beside a book like a companion volume.

Oh well, it was inevitable; they turned down the exact aisle where I hid. They walked halfway down where they spotted me. "Kathy?" Lois said, "Is that you?"

I turned, red-faced, like a child with her hand in the cookie jar. The Lord always has the last laugh—"Where can I go from your wisdom? From your presence where can I flee?" (Psalm 139:7)

Needless to say, when I shared my prayer and God's peculiar answer with her, she gave me a big hug. She'd been in the same place long ago and knew just what to say. The next week I was off with her to Al-Anon. The group was a saving grace for me, and its value superseded any repercussions from my family. Without that group, I would have continued on the merry-go-round of worry and self-blame that families of alcoholics ride.

Romans 8:28, "We know that all things work together for the good of those who are called according to His purpose," was proved again by the repercussions from my decision. *My big step overflowed like a waterfall into the life of another person close to me.*

A dear friend of mine who was a pastor in another community struggled daily with alcohol himself. He was a wonderful man, and only those close to him were aware of the *devil* that plagued him. Unknowingly, I had sought him out many times by mail or phone with my worries. He guided me with his great spiritual and practical advice. When I shared that I had joined Al-Anon, somehow in God's mysterious way, he opened his heart to the Lord's beckoning voice and joined AA. When he told his congregation that he was an alcoholic, he spoke about the friend who gave him the courage to finally get help for himself.

Whenever I think of this story, I feel an awesome tenderness in my heart. Curiously enough, when I asked for guidance about what reflection to work on next, not only did I find a small painting of marsh marigolds that Lois had painted for me, but also, in doing a long-needed job of sorting papers and cards I have kept, I found a letter this dear pastor wrote to me when he retired. In it he states, "I want to thank you for being part of my *Last Hurrah* and for all you did … for me in the past years. Thank you for everything— especially the inspiration you have given me …"

So God used Lois to inadvertently change the lives of two people, and she and I became good friends.

Over the Back Fence

Last year, at Christmastime, I received my annual Christmas letter from Katherine. Her mother had finally died at the grand old age of 101. I had no doubt in my mind that the reason she had lived so long was due to the faithful kindness of her daughter, who loved the Lord and exhibited that love in caring for others.

Katherine lived just over the fence on the street parallel to mine. She was another example of the *Gracious Woman* of Proverbs 31. Christ was the center of her life. In addition, she had a large, bright, and talented family; kept a lovely home, garden, and yard; worked diligently for her church; and still took the time to be there for her neighbors. I especially enjoyed her dry humor and little witticisms.

From her example I learned the importance of expecting the best from your children and having the faith that they will not let you down. Her *do your best* was a great slogan. I easily incorporated it into my habitual expectations for my own children, and it paid off. With every assignment and every report card, I asked, "Did you do your best?" They knew that was all I asked of them, and they delivered. Then, later, when I returned to teaching, I took Katherine's principle into my classroom too. "I know you will do your best!" I frequently told my students and again it paid off: nothing expected, nothing gained … high expectations, high results.

Later, at one job interview, one of the interviewers in the group asked me how I managed as a single parent to have such well-adjusted, talented children. At the time I thought that a question about my personal life was not appropriate, but nonetheless I answered, "I just ask them to do their best." All in the room gaped at me like I'd stumbled on some strange idea. I know that the Lord put Katherine's example in my heart, and hopefully my children, now parents themselves, will carry on with this proven philosophy.

Roses for Remembrance

When I see my first spring robin, I always think of Ellie, who lived in a bright little house two blocks over. She made it her specific goal to see the first robin in our little community. Then, she blissfully informed everyone who came her way, that spring had arrived. Hope for sunny days and bright flowers changed her whole demeanor. As the robin is a faithful sign of spring, so Ellie represented the spirit of faithfulness to the friends that she gathered into her humble heart.

Ellie was often misunderstood. A serious person, she spent much time thinking and philosophizing about the events that surrounded her. It took time for her to express her inward musings. As a result, as is the case with many sages, few had the patience to listen and thus thought her just another eccentric. I think we became friends because I was willing to explore ideas with her and respond to her innermost thoughts. She taught me to be a listener.

We also shared many spiritual discussions in her bright kitchen. Ellie kept a notebook while she read her daily readings and would refer to something that had touched her heart. Then we'd discuss the idea for some time amidst the folding of laundry, the stirring of simmering soups or sauces, and the frequent interruptions of our playing children.

Being young in the Lord and still learning, we'd often do little childlike spiritual things like open our Bibles just to see where we would land and see if the Lord had something to say to us. One time, Ellie was feeling frustrated with things and asked, "What are you telling me, Lord?" She opened a modern translation (similar in idea to today's *Message Bible*) and put her finger down. The passage read, "I am not trying to tell you anything ..." I've never forgotten that incident, as it always makes me laugh. What a lesson was taught that day about thinking too much, instead of going with the flow of trusting God to carry us through.

Ellie loved St. Therese of Lisieux (a French Carmelite nun in the Catholic tradition). Roses are associated with her, and she is called the *Little Flower*. Often, as I tend my rose garden, I think of Ellie and occasionally send her a card with roses on it. Years have passed, and I know that if I call Ellie today with a need or a prayer request, she will respond as if I were sitting at her table. She is a fine example of a loyal and faithful friend.

Thank you, Lois, Ellie, and Katherine for
giving me courage, strategies, and gracious
understandings that I apply to my everyday life.

Prayer

Glorious Lord, how many different people walk our pilgrimage with us? The body of Christ is so available to us if we just look with the eyes of faith. It is all so simple, and yet we make it hard. Lord, open our eyes to see. Open our hearts to understand. Open our minds to reap your abundant wisdom and give it to each other. Open our hands to help. Let us never think for a moment that we can do this life journey alone. Thank You for being Savior and our lifelong companion. Thank You for the people You send into our lives at just the right times. Amen.

Body of Christ

Before I was even a thought, you knew me, Lord.
On the day I was born, you placed your angel by my
shoulder.
Divine wisdom … just a call away, you mold me with
Yearning that I will always answer your call on my life.

On this journey
Friends fold like soft blankets into the arms of my heart.

Come along—
Hold my hand and grasp another until we make a love
circle
Right in the everydayness of life.
In joy and sorrow, strength and weakness,
Some anointed person speaks your wisdom, Lord.
Together the **I** becomes a **we** … this body of Christ.

Questions to contemplate or discuss:

1. (*The Fleece*) Have you been involved in a support group? How did it help you? If not, take some time to look into a support group for your information … this new found knowledge might be helpful to someone who crosses your path in the future.

2. (*Over the Back Fence*) Reflect on words or phrases that you've incorporated into your vocabulary. Where did they come from? … Home? … School? … A friend? Share or write about one or more of these ideas and how it impacts your life.

3. (*Roses for Remembrance*) What is involved in being a good listener? Are there others you know who may have wisdom to share if you give them the time to express themselves?

4. Think about what the body of Christ means to you … then discuss or write about it.

Scripture readings/reflections:

1. Romans: chapter 12
2. 2 Timothy 1:1–14
3. Philemon

A story to read: "The Giving Tree," by Shel Silverstein.

A wonderful modern-day children's classic about the meaning of true love.

Personal Reflections

Innocence

At the same hour Jesus rejoiced in the Holy
Spirit and said, "I thank you, Father, Lord
of heaven and earth, because you have
hidden these things from the wise and the
intelligent and have revealed them to infants;
yes, Father, for such was your gracious will."
(Luke 10:21 RSV)

Our neighborhood sported a motley crew of children of all
ages. Like a great bowl of cookie dough, they all blended
together ready to be fashioned into the people God planned
them to be. They played together, watched over and protected
each other, and added their share of worry-wrinkles to their
mothers' faces. When all was said and done, it was an ideal
place to bring up a child.

A small creek ran between several of our homes. It was
an important gathering place for all the children. Minnows
and crayfish lived in the water. Large rocks provided
stepping stones to ford the creek. The bridges had metal
railings ideal for hanging upside down, thus providing
temptation for fearless kids and anxiety for their moms.
In the winter, this creek provided a place for little people
to ice skate.

The newspaper photographer seemed to like our neighborhood. I have one newspaper picture of an older child helping a little one stand up on ice skates in a precarious pose in the frozen creek on a winter day. Another spring picture appeared in the paper of two of the little girls hanging, heads down, hair streaming and smiles wide, as their legs and arms grasped the bridge railing.

Because water is always a big attraction with young ones, hardly a summer day passed without activity in that creek. Painting stones was popular, along with finding the best stone to write on the sidewalk with. Stone skipping, mud pies, fishing (with cans of course), and make-believe were welcome invitations from *Old Father Creek*. All manner of imaginative play lingered around the water rivulets. One summer, several little boys decided to set up a business scheme.

As I mentioned before, crayfish were abundant in the shady nooks of the creek. Unbeknownst to their mothers, several of the little boys decided to catch crayfish and sell them to Anna's husband. Suddenly, the usually grumpy old man who thought children shouldn't be seen *or* heard became friendly. Motherly antennas were just on the verge of going up, when, again, a reporter just happened by on a balmy afternoon and asked the boys what they were doing. The three young culprits got their picture in the paper engaged in their crayfish scam. Soon the prolific trade of *bait for money* came to a halt, as did the *secret* trips to the corner store to spend their earnings. The neighborhood *mafia* was tamed and a newly formed group emerged. An apt name for the new enterprise might have been *kind boys catch free crayfish for dear old neighborhood fisherman* … hopefully the culprits learned a lesson.

My son walked home from kindergarten one day right through the creek. I watched him soaking his brand new school shoes. When he came in all wet from the shins down, I innocently asked him how he got so wet. Without a pause, he said, "Well, mom, there was this puddle and it just kind of jumped up on me."

"Interesting," I replied as I hid my face and stifled a chortle.

The water was not the only child-gift in our special corner of the world. The woods that sauntered up the hill behind Grace's house were preceded by a wetland, which sported wildlife and occasional feasts of flowers. One of the wooded paths led to an old, no longer used cemetery. It was in good repair, and from that hilly spot, you could see for a long way over the hills and dales. It was a nice place to end a hike and have a bagged lunch. It was also a good teaching spot for life and death discussions. Then, before starting back home, the little ones enjoyed rolling down the sides of the big hill just beyond the gravestones. We'd walk home and pick wildflowers on the way.

Grace had shown all the kids the marsh marigolds (cowslips) that bloomed in May. The little ones would get together on Mother's Day morning, quietly slipping out of their houses with a "be right back," and traipse off to the wetland to pick bouquets for us. In addition, they usually grabbed a few lilacs from an abundant bush on the way home. (Mother's Day never goes by for me without memories of those *secret* trips - one of those warm heart-memories.)

From morning until night there was action on our little street. The long sidewalks were perfect for tricycle and Big Wheel riding. Roller skating was still popular, and the street was usually quiet enough for young bikers to experiment without their training wheels. The protective school age crowd was always on hand to comfort the fallen and encourage the hesitant.

My backyard was perfect for baseball. It wasn't long before all the grass at first, second, third, and home bases, along with the pitcher's mound, were only a memory. My garden and the creek were foul ball territory, while a ball hit over the creek in the back was a home run. The *team* ranged from three-year-olds to teenagers and was always good for a good belly chuckle. Often, when *serious* baseball was called for, the *big* boys would pick a few of the younger, more skilled little ones. With permission, they'd take them off for some *real* baseball at the schoolyard. The school was within walking distance with lots of Little League ball fields to use. It also sported a *modern* wooden playground with all of its myriad mazes, nooks, and crannies.

One of my favorite memories from my own backyard happened on a summer day. It must have been naptime, as it was pretty quiet out. Two of the neighborhood boys had passed into adolescence and had started to loosen the bonds with the younger crew. I was in the kitchen washing dishes and just happened to look out my back door window. There, sitting in the sandbox, were those two strapping fourteen-year-olds playing with the sand toys. I kept quiet, watching and laughing inwardly. They were still just little boys in big bodies.

The girls loved to dress up and waddle up and down the street with their mothers' heels on, funny purses bulging with treasures adorning their arms and hats that slid down to their noses and hid their eyes. Naturally the boys tried to rankle them, always seeming to forget that yesterday that same little group of ladies had given them a run for their money on the baseball diamond. The *sweet* little girls' purses were good weapons and kept their tormentors at a distance.

All the moms in the neighborhood took turns watching the whole crew from time to time to give each other breaks. One morning, I listened to *Focus on the Family*. Dr. James Dobson was giving advice to young mothers. He said that if you needed a break, the bathroom was one of the places where children would often leave you alone for awhile. With four little ones, I grabbed on to this great advice. I started putting a book or two beside the toilet and staying for just a tad longer on my visits. One sunny day, while my kids were happily playing at the neighbor's, I decided to take the advice a bit farther and have a nice quiet bath. I had settled myself in for some peaceful moments when I heard a noise coming up the stairs. Naturally I thought that my kids were home early.

"Mom," one of them called.

"I'm in here," I dutifully called back.

Then, to my chagrin, my kids plus at least eight of the

neighbors' kids burst into the bathroom to visit me. James Dobson needed to add one more sentence to his advice: *Be sure the door is locked.*

That event is a memory that always makes me laugh, but the greatest thing about the whole incident was that the kids didn't think anything about it. I was just another of their *moms* doing a natural thing.

Because I was there for a good ten years, I watched several of the young ones grow from childhood to high school and a couple even to college age. As they grew older, each woman in our little body of Christ served a new role in the now maturing eyes of these young adults. Some came to us for help and direction, others watched our kids, and most went through the normal awkwardness that accompanies adolescence. Suddenly, before our eyes, a thin gawky little girl would turn into a comely young lady, while the guys graduated from Matchbox cars to revving engines.

Remarkably, these teens stayed connected to those who were still just *little.* It wasn't unusual to see one or more of them taking time to help one of the little ones across the street or picking up a sad and hurting child who had fallen off a bike. I've always thought that because they watched the nurturing that the women on our street gave to each other, they learned by example the gift of kindness … especially for those who are dependent and helpless. I am eternally grateful that my children had their start in such a fine neighborhood.

One last story bears telling. My last years in this community, I was a single parent. While I spent time seeking guidance for my future, this great group of neighbors took special care of my children and me. *Surrogate fathers* were there for the boys, and teenagers chipped in to help with outdoor chores too hard for me. One day I asked Sophie's son, Ryan, to plow my garden. He came over with a cultivator and blithely started the job.

A short time later there was a great commotion. I heard a loud noise, and several feet beat up the porch stairs, calling me as they rushed through the door. I ran out, and there in the middle of the garden was Ryan propped precariously atop a large hole. His machine was nowhere in sight. He looked at me in a daze, and as the crowd got larger, he dragged himself to his feet … looking down in amazement.

Unbeknownst to me, long before the village sewer was put in, the area under my garden had been a dry well. It sighed under the pressure of ten years of gardening, and poor Ryan just happened to be the recipient of the proverbial straw that broke the camel's back. I was so embarrassed, but thank God, Ryan was not hurt. He looked so funny. It is one of those memories that bring laughter into my heart. He was such a great sport. He sure doesn't fall into holes anymore. He has a wonderful ministry and is a great father. I think he probably had the groundwork for his future laid out for him in my little garden.

There was a small miracle that happened that day too. Usually Anna's husband, well into his eighties, tilled my garden for me. If I remember right, he was sick that week. Of course, God's perfect plan was at work, and in this case, I don't even like to think what might have happened if that dear old man had had a dry well disaster. Like all the wonderful memories I have of the children, this is another special one.

Thank you all … you great kids all grown
up now. May you remember your roots
and pass that wisdom on to others.

Prayer

Lord, You are so gracious. You place us in just the right places at just the right times in our lives. We don't always see or understand why we are there until much later as we reflect and see Your purpose. Help us, Lord, to trust in You and listen. When we see children, help us to realize what an important part we have in their nurturing, even in simple ways like a kind word or a gentle smile. Put on our hearts a burden for the young so that we will always pray for their guidance in a complicated world. Lord, bless the children. Amen.

Enchantment

Like some enchanted whirlwind,
Our children change and grow
So fast …
Years cascade like a waterfall,
Flowing swiftly over some
Timeless mountaintop ridge just beyond our reach.
We can't quite catch them … they're not our own to keep.
Passing … passing quickly by,
We grab at the memories.
They fill our hearts with picture-stories …
Rewinding and replaying again and again
O'er our long years we watch as
The Gift Givers
Give to another …
This enchanted whirlwind of life.
Passing … passing quickly by
In someone else's time … forever …
Till He comes to take us home.
Hush … hear new life whispering, "I'm here … Hello."

Questions to contemplate or discuss:

1. Children's stories are always dear to our hearts. Think about or share one or more of your special memories of the children you nurtured or grew up with.

2. Single parenting is a daunting task, and children of single parents often need extra encouragement. Can I be a surrogate mother to a young person in my neighborhood that is being raised by a father? Would my husband or brother be willing to share some of his skills with a child who is being reared by a mother?

3. How much do I encourage my children to play outside and explore what nature has to offer?

4. If I am working, do I make the effort to expose my children to nature centers or hike with them in the woods?

5. Single adults have a great gift to give by sharing their time with needy children or with the children of single parents. (My children have a wonderful *auntie* who has always been there for them, as well as an encouragement to me.) Is this something I could try?

Scripture readings/reflections:

1. Psalm 127
2. Matthew 18:1–6
3. Luke 2:51–52

Something to write:

Write the story you shared in #1 above. Give it to your child or children in a specially decorated folder or frame for a birthday present.

Personal Reflections

Afterword

The Wonder of It All

Yes, those were simpler times … times God ordained for me. I look back in grateful amazement on those years lived in the shelter of so many wonderful women. They gave me the nurturing time I needed to face the challenging years that came next in the lives of my children and me. Their gifts prepared me to be a single parent and never lose sight of God as the Father in our little family. I took the wisdom learned in that neighborhood with me into the classroom at school as well as into the classroom of life. Much later, when God placed a special man in my life, their wisdom taught me to be a better wife.

We now live in a different time. Neighborhoods are quiet now for most of the day. Children are nurtured at day care centers, and in some neighborhoods, people hardly know anyone beyond their next-door neighbor. Technology makes communication instant and continuous, but not necessarily personal. Cell phones connect us to each other like giant labyrinthine strings. The world has become our neighborhood. Despite all of these changes, I believe the body of Christ will continue to work together in new ways. It may seem unfathomable to those of us who nurtured each other in kitchens, on front porches, and over a phone's long extension cord, but nonetheless, the Holy Spirit is always at work.

> "I am about to do a new thing, now it springs
> forth, do you not perceive it? I will make a way
> in the wilderness and rivers in the desert."
> (Isaiah 43:19 RSV)

When I am tempted to linger over the past, I stop myself, remembering that God is in control. Then, hopefully, I look around me to notice that, like a circle, God calls all things back to himself. I notice that many of the gorgeous new homes have huge front porches with inviting rocking chairs. I notice that many little groups of women meet to share Scripture and talk over tea or coffee. I notice the number of moms who've chosen to stay home and teach their own children, then meet in networks with other like-minded ladies.

I marvel at the return to things that, in our simpler time, we took for granted. Craft stores have sprung up like flower patches everywhere, and classes invite women to meet and learn crafting or sewing together. Scrapbooking groups share picture ideas and inadvertently give advice through shared experience. Quilt making itself is so simplified with the advent of new machine technology that those who love quilting can complete a beautiful piece of work in less time.

In my area, many women get together to share this gift and make quilts for those who are in need.

Groups like MOPS (Mothers of Pre-Schoolers) have popped up across the country, filling the need of young mothers to share their gifts and frustrations while their children play together under the supervision of volunteers.

I went with my daughter and her children on a wonderful field trip especially designed for homeschoolers. The guide had been a home school mom herself and was well versed in the needs of her little group. I enjoyed the chitchat of the moms as they shared various ideas they were trying with their students, as well as the challenges they faced.

Women need women. Women need friendship and talk. Women can help other women on their way to be better wives, mothers, and single adults. Most important, women need Christ, and once they have Him, they are a loving helpful inspiration to each other. Amen!

Addendum

Names with a Message

I chose names for my friends that I thought most represented their gifts to me and to others.

Grace (Wonder): When I think of the name Grace, I think of the continuous ways God blesses us with His grace. The Grace of my story blessed us with her unwavering presence and availability to each of us. Her open home and her vast knowledge gave us wonder to explore and wisdom to experience.

Julia (Service): The common meaning of Julia is *youthful*. My Julia was an older woman with a youthful spirit. She was someone to emulate as each of us grows older. She had such a good attitude and did not let her age stand in her way.

Ruth (Determination): One of the less common meanings of Ruth is *to join together*. My Ruth, despite her great challenges, joined our neighborhood together in caring for someone less fortunate. She also gathered us together to teach us how important it is to be a caring community, working and laughing in Christ.

Anna (Humor): My neighbor Anna was a gracious woman to me. She was able to accept things as they were and made the most of living with a cantankerous husband. She watched out for me and my children and told me gently, but frankly, when she saw things that were amiss. I loved laughing with her as she waited, like Anna in Luke's account of the presentation of Jesus, to go peacefully to see her Savior.

May (Compassion): May is the month of flowers and leaves and birds babbling in glee. It is a wistful month, and my May was a wistful person. In the world where she lived, all was well … all was perfection and peace. I know it was not a real world, but it was a place that took her away from the fearful place of reality. So, with love, I gave her the name that I feel our loving God might have chosen for her.

Sophie (Wisdom): Sophie is and always will be wisdom to me … a wise friend, a wise wife and mother. She was also wise enough to laugh at the bumps in the road that come our way as we walk with the Lord and grow.

Emma (The In and Outers): The German meaning of Emma is *industrious*. This name suits my Emma to a tee. She was always busy and trying new things.

Lenora (The In and Outers): I picked this wonderful old-fashioned name for a wonderful *old-fashioned* lady … a glimpse of the past in the rush of the present.

Lucy (The In and Outers): - Lucy's name is the name for someone *light-spirited*, and she was. I can still see her breezing in and out of our days.

Lois (The Fleece): The name Lois occurs in the New Testament (2 Timothy 1:5) as the name of Timothy's grandmother, in whom dwelt *unfeigned faith*. I think this definition speaks for my friend.

Katherine (Over the Back Fence): There are many pages in the book *Girls' Christian Names** devoted to the name Katherine. The common meaning is *pure,* and that applies to my friend, but I would add some of the other meanings: beauty, grace, and intellectual devotion. Year after year, when I receive her Christmas letter, I see the fruits of her faith and labors reflected in her inspiring Christian letters.

Ellie (Roses for Remembrance): The name Ellie is associated with *light*. Whenever my Ellie received a new spiritual understanding, she couldn't wait to share her enlightenment with me. In addition, her kitchen was always light, as it has multiple windows, making it enjoyable to share coffee at her cozy table.

Bibliography

*Swan, Helena. *Girls' Christian Names: Their History, Meaning and Association*. Tokyo: Charles E. Tuttle and Co.: reprinted 1973, copyright 1900. 327-335.

About the Author:

Kathleen McDonald is a freelance writer, poet, and teacher who holds a BS and MS degree in Education from the State University of New York at Cortland. Her teaching experience includes public and private school, teaching adults and children, as well as planning and implementing curriculum for Christian and public education. She has had several articles and poems published. Presently she is working fulltime on her writing.

In addition to her book of reflections on women's friendship, she is putting the finishing touches on her first novel, has completed three children's book manuscripts, and hopes to compile her poetry into an anthology. She fashions much of her writing from the word sketches and poetry that fill her journals.

Mrs. McDonald, a mother and grandmother, lives with her husband in Bath, New York. Aside from her passion for writing and reading, she is active in her church; belongs to a Bible study group; dabbles in art; and enjoys scrapbooking, card making, and gardening. She loves film, music, and travel and, of course, delights in her grandchildren.